night myths •

• before the body

night myths •

• before the body

poems

abi pollokoff

Red Hen Press | *Pasadena, CA*

Cover art: *Rosemary's Garden Flowers,* 2015, by Rachel Dein

Library of Congress Cataloging-in-Publication Data

Names: Pollokoff, Abi, author.
Title: Night myths · · before the body / Abi Pollokoff.
Description: First edition. | Pasadena, CA: Red Hen Press, 2025.
Identifiers: LCCN 2024018639 (print) | LCCN 2024018640 (ebook) | ISBN 9781636281971 (trade paperback) |
  ISBN 9781636281995 (hardcover) | ISBN 9781636281988 (ebook)
Subjects: LCGFT: Poetry.
Classification: LCC PS3616.O56967 N54 2025 (print) | LCC PS3616.O56967
  (ebook) | DDC 811/.6—dc23/eng/20240719
LC record available at https://lccn.loc.gov/2024018639
LC ebook record available at https://lccn.loc.gov/2024018640

The National Endowment for the Arts, the Los Angeles County Arts Commission, the Ahmanson Foundation, the Dwight Stuart Youth Fund, the Max Factor Family Foundation, the Pasadena Tournament of Roses Foundation, the Pasadena Arts & Culture Commission and the City of Pasadena Cultural Affairs Division, the City of Los Angeles Department of Cultural Affairs, the Audrey & Sydney Irmas Charitable Foundation, the Meta & George Rosenberg Foundation, the Albert and Elaine Borchard Foundation, the Adams Family Foundation, Amazon Literary Partnership, the Sam Francis Foundation, and the Mara W. Breech Foundation partially support Red Hen Press.

First Edition
Published by Red Hen Press
www.redhen.org

to all the women who helped me find my way

& to all the women still finding theirs

Contents

●

●

● ●

•

•

•

"the dark is thin tonight a blue vein showing its pulse please advise"
—Rusty Morrison

a long vulnerability of paper & consciousness
found

the shape you're in   projected interchangeably
            back to body
                              our vernacular diagrams
                              at once authentic & suspended:

eyes, transparencies   the intimate immigrant
            of reinvention

you describe porosity:
            palms like the radiant taste of granite dust
            mouth like the tunnel committed to narrative
            the throat: steel-ribbed vastness
                        run-on sentences based in witness

break open these simultaneous roles   *this concept*

      logistically it is a kind of spandex language

            are we but lying?
                  mouth with their mists of self-making
                  throat cut with fragrance
                  palms: this edge of "please"   of nothing

                                                hands in old silk

every day we are told to fear our name   the first compass
every day we tilt back to words as they seek new syntaxes

                                          prosperous together

each generation has music   a degree of glass
      that digs into starker image

      the shape you're in   aerial
         the personal space

                 a hundred palms falling

:

cross your legs uncross your legs cross your legs uncross your legs cross your legs
uncross your legs sit still & say hello   *the stiller the louder*

island sided

in the middle of expanse. what it means to be. alone on
a rowboat. to row. us surrounded. in stretching
silhouettes of. the shadows of. pine strata. birches. lilies
comprising islands where. are the islands. edged in rocks
we're. rocking through. our terror of. rocks how loud
our. terror how. loud the crunch of. rocks glinting. with
lilies. little flecks. of light. of our surfaces. & in the water
below little. flecks of light. the plankton. endless wells.
of mica glinting. over the edge of. the rowboat we're.
rowing we're. rowing we're. rowing through. a blink of.
moonlight blinding a. light as dense. as darkness.

                        blind the moon. with
the blink of. a lighthouse. lighting the moon's. plunge.
to the placid. shadows steeling the. rowboat surrounded.
with rocks &. light &. underneath a. glowing crush of.
phosphorus unsleeping. a deception in. water &. the
discomfort of. moonlight. lilies under oars &. density of.
swallowed water. swallowed oars. pressure weakened
by. the wake of. the boat we're rowing. we're rowing.
we're rowing. we're rowing. i wonder are we. rowing.
any closer to the buoy

the auction

i woke up this morning with seagulls encased inside me

& i said, "here   this is what i have to offer"
      the seagulls preened & prodded

          & you said, "do you have anything for sale?"
& i said, "here take these seagulls   they're inside me"

you looked at the skin encasing them   as the seagulls preened & prodded
     & you said, "how will you set them free   for me?"

& i said, "i will run them out   through my knees"
      the seagulls preened & prodded   they knew they were for sale

& you said, "i am not too fond of knees

                        i am too consumed
                            in your wrists"

:

cross your legs uncross your legs cross your legs uncross your legs cross your legs uncross
your legs don't be cross no wonder   the ankle sits in such a curved question mark
*   knee greater   or less than*

wildflower mythology

first there was
                            a lady

        stemwrapped &
                                rooted

    •

wide open & spinning
            in wildflowers   in gold threads
                                soilsoaked
            her display

●

these casual gifts

                     her wildflowers

●

& the wildflowers

                        their tendencies

         to consume breezes
         to sip breath

•

all in good breeding

                              the wildflowers   the lady

•

        wildflowers
                    slipped into their stems

            greening just   at the throat

•

the lady skirts
                    the wildflowers
            afraid of their tendencies

                                        her good breeding

•

              the lady's skirts

                              goldthreaded now

wildflowers

                       catching patterns in breezes

•

pulling up wildflowers

              gold at the root

                    this soilsoaked lady

                green in disarray

•

         breezes, wheedling

                      with stolen tongues

the wildflowers' good breeding

                    the lady's display

•

shadowplucked, the wildflowers

—a falter at the edge of breath—
missing breezes

•

the lady   the wildflowers

their frail cacophonies
emptying

their throats
their soundless stems

billow & pulse

wide open in the meadow, a
shell in the greenspeak. wide
open & spinning in it.

gold thread spinning here, gold
heads tipsy. gold thread on the
arm & gold thread in the eye:
glisten & flicker & glisten &
gleam.

wingkissed & airy, i'm full up
in lilies. all harken & bloom. all
sunnery.

burrow in the toes & take root:
minute after minute after
month. don't leave the
windwatch, don't leave the furl.
fingers in flicker & display. in
parity & pearl the little nailbeds,
settled & stretched. palms
bedded down with terrain, all
tucked in & gleaming.

•

those toes are rooted now.
bone, something to keep
covered. the skin: a mesh with
its own weakness.

pestilence & process: virus in
the touch of the earth, all soaked
in & sobbing. see it & retreat.
see it & believe. the body is the
muscle & the dirtstrain. the
muscle strains & splinters.

this is the body being soaked
up. this is the body being
soaped in. this is body being
pulled down, pushing out its
skin & pruning. falling
skincaved into granite &
dismay. this is the body rejecting
itself.

what's silent. what's screaming.
this, the self's screech &
summon.

the minute & the month take
the same time: breath only one
breath, only one breach.

•

in this always assuming state:
tongue all twisted up about
itself. so many things in the
body, all sucked up from
below. so many things in the
body, so many things to cave it.
hard things & soft things. hard
things & soft things. hard things
& soft things all up the spine.

so: self-diagnose.   self-
medicate.   self-mediate.
measure & miss.measure &
miss. measure & measure
again. remind the self to be
human. remind the self to be
animal. tell the self to be tame.
grow a little.

a breeze in the breath. a music
now, what the body is made of.
breathe some life into the spine
& willow through it. bend &
don't break. beseech. beseech
beseech. beseech.

•

wide open in the meadow, self
grows out the self. goldthreaded,
the animal body. the human one:
wingkissed. airy. i—we—all full
up in lilies. what aroma here,
what odor. virus in the touch of
us, unboned & burning.

toes in the row of earth: all full up
with dirt & willow. love the
breeze of it, a disappearing act.
our terroir, plucked & dried. this
body is made of all these
beautiful dead things, all wormed
up. all wriggling. stretch into the
rustle here: ruby in the root. ruby
on the brow. ruby is the pebble &
the sweat.

so soundless, this body, bedded
down with nettles. all worked out
as something to grow, to gather.
the madness is a muscle,
stretched & tensing. all verbed
out. all swallowing. all worked
out, the root & rush of us now, all
spineplucked & empty—what
toes. what root. what vertebrae.

:

cross your legs uncross your legs cross your legs uncross your legs cross your legs
uncross your   *these withered appendages all dried up &*
prickling   *no toe touch towing the legs along*   *along these*

:

these synaptic passages   reveal certain digital deaths   electric
          chromatic isotopes   wrists all bluechromed in the low neon light
throat   spine spindled down to conjunction   of rings & time

particular reminders when prayers for the body aren't enough

when dusty purple fruits breathe in
the sunsets & smog of their cityscapes:
                    that's the answer

branches dangle down splintering poles
& fenceposts & abandoned pianos
                    into gestures of hurry & freeze

                            who makes this body what it is
                    what makes this body what it's made of

into questions of dusk & breath & billow
& palm & squeeze & pulse & pluck & ooze

        with such silhouettes, what gets left when light

                            enters the room?

            the fruits' bursted juices all over an unsuspecting wrist

all over city corners   stretch
                               hold
                               hurry

        dusky purple veins branch a map of smoke & defiance

                    throats in yellow light

flick away dust from the skin you've seen before
            unbidden orbits: the body wrapped & unwrapped
                    the body frozen   in its glassy musics

it's not a question of streets or piano keys

it's not a question to fill veins with tendrils of carved bark

         & wrapped & unwrapped

when the body's wrappings strip themselves into collage of
gummed muscle   marrowly melting into

pinking bone   here's a question:
         is the body swallowed in fabric to hide

                 or to hold it

        along the fenceline
            the headiness of plums

in shadow in
        recline
        lean into it

intertwine branches with every last shadow
        every particle of smog

watch the body   *hurry—*
     watch the body—

:

cross your legs uncross your legs cross your legs uncross your legs cross your legs uncross your legs tell yourself   stand up   eat the plum & spit the pits   slip & stick them under toes to sprout

**to live in ignorance is
exactly what**

an ageless geography, this
dizzying sisyphus that defines
the tremor of knots & water. at
the wrist, a turning away. at the
knee, a slip toward the ankle.
tide corroded by its own salt
into tangled driplight.

the glinting the glinting the
glinting oh the lily golden
against the day & what's
hungered. against the
birchhymned absence shorn of
breath & bismuth.

for the wrist pressed into
compass glass, crystal dinging
with what's lost. for the excess
of plums & gulls that tear
the tender   flesh. for the
unraveling   into   abdication.
there's nothing

here to covet. of what's been
asked across the oscillating
apsis
        across the edge of synapse
which question is left to
summon?

all strung out in axes,
        asp & aspen both sense the
same direction.

:

along these synaptic passages a living rock   the one that laughs in the light   the one that's pushed into furrow when plowed   cross your legs uncross your legs cross your legs uncross your legs cross your legs uncross your legs be tree be grass be rock

if the mirror

in its gilded frame

                                         beheld the body's greeneries   something

lovely:

                a face of leisure

                a leaning in   the neck's question

nothing more

                              than a slung shoulder

                a slipped stem into   a gilded vase

                                                    an unstrung bodice

                                                                          would it be

the lady or the thread
                    tucking itself into   a stretching fog

                    throating out a call
          or reply
                                                             it's a lovely thing

to be the mirror
     to be the lady

                              & with the neck in repose
                         what's the throat to do

:

these synaptic passages reveal   *certain binary clefts*   *certain*
doctrines of cellular isthmus   *ecstatic uncoupling*
    crossuncross   *crossuncross*   *un-*

a walk in the woods

a scarstitched birch & its lilies
taken to the roots & the moon &
two foottrails : night knows
nothing of the slip of its bark all
daycurled & dreaming

& in canopy's throat where
we're walking how much time
will it take : how many acorns
stepped into moss to abandon
day's sleeping ghosts : to
abandon aspen to the acorns to
the daydrenched lilies: to
relinquish petal & pistil to
night's silvering curiosities

•

the woods here shiver into their
limbs : we shiver into the shape
of birch trees rubbing off their
peels as if it were hard to unskin
the self : as if birches didn't strip
down to their wrists

the moon skims the mane of the
woods & waits to rub its
beckoned neck & we are half
unbreached of our knees & we
are half numbed & the acorns
how many undermossed &
shivering

•

& trailing we tighten our teeth
into what shadows these
underbellies : this circling
silence below the birchbased
lilies below the moss & the
aspen silent as we stop
pretending to lead the way into
ourselves & into other people

the insistence of knuckles & the
way they bud out of finger's
stretch : we're more than this
grasp & clench : we're more
than this trail in the speechless
night

•

& hurrying what faces lie above
ours what breezes corroded at
the knee how much time will it
take to emerge as anything
other than
>   lily
>   lily
>   lily
>   lily

& how to emerge anything but
straightspined & tense arms
raised to scarstitched birches &
aspen & the moon & lilies &
birches & aspen & the moon

>   all siltfaced & seething

:

cross your legs uncross your legs cross your legs uncross your legs uncross your legs
along these synaptic passages   a ridge of bonesap   a slick of
history's ribbing   along these synaptic passages the seeking of some
semantic branch   or root

:

name yourself   something spring   cross   seed
     uncross   & seedling   crossuncross   bloomling   &
bloom

to forest is to hide a woman

i have this. body & they tell me. it is. it is the body of a
woman they tell. me it is the body. of woman but they
do not. tell me how. to woman. they tell me how. do
you do how. do you woman. or you.   how
do i.

i swarm. myself to be a. body. to become. a woman i
am. leeching woman lisping & claiming. a name. for
which i do. not ask i do not ask. to woman i do not want.
to quiver i. want. to know what my insides are. i want.
to know what. is a woman.

•

i want to know how. my insides are i. want to catch the dripping. light of stained. glass hanging from. rafters. & drink it into. me. hold it. hold it close to. breezes &. sing a little. in the light. don't make light

of this please breath. look. closer. i parcel out. my tongue to. please. parcel i parcel this. is my body without. a tongue. this stained. glass tongue. look closer. look & eye. the light leeching. through it.

•

its names. its women leeching & lisping after. their bodies their. insides. these tracts i. shelter. i am. shelter & dismay. i am. correct. i must correct my. categories my. cavities my. insides parcel. them out this. much body that. much woman i must. catch the dripping glass. stained light. leeching.

over rafters like. the moth i am. to woman i. moth over rafters in. breezes as. missile i. slip skinned into. birches into. aspen i. skin my skin. with spiderwebs. insides left. hanging. no one tongued. to notice. i am birch i. am forest i. vein slender i. birch swiftly i.

•

aspen into forest i. veined & dripping this. stand my.
forest my. insides my. bark. together painted into. glass
frames. claiming sight. claiming rafters to hold. this
body. together where. is the woman i. see only birch see.
only aspen see. forest &.

it is night there.

:

cross your legs uncross your legs cross your legs uncross your legs cross your legs
uncross your legs look up & shhhh   *primjawed & tongueless*
    tightshinned & kickless   *slackpalmed & slapless*
    little hollow hands grafting pixel   *to shadow*

the hearth no longer a hallowed frame   *i found*

a plague of seagulls there
gripping the stygian tryst, a tug
ever downwards   ever

knees supplicant   as birches
pneumatized wingbones,   spent sepals dreaming of blooms

is this what it's like
to have a matchstick?
i could certainly   imagine

reading ashes like tea leaves

wingbreeze left every scavenge of carbon & stem
mantel both mantel & memory

:

shadow as in stripe as in rib as in ridge as in furrow as in brow as in coolclothed &
trembling   as in all the revel   all the reveal

:

cross your legs uncross your legs cross your legs uncross your legs cross your legs
uncross your legs   shadow as in tremor
      as in electric treble   a slight shakin—   moveme—
            nervousness   or excitement   a slight quake

7:28 PM: above the river the bridge   the bridge

& then there's a bee in the hand:

buzz nuzzled into skin   skin
a muzzle   when instinct clenches
                        & lily when fingers release   now

all pink & blooming with sting   sting
                        that rips the body   from the body
                                                                            that swells

                of pulse   & insistence

above sun-stained bricks: bricks
belligerent   in their heat in their   fortitude
        in their inability   to abandon post

& dive in the water below   bellowing
                                                                            river

            to unpluck reflection   or mellow
                        into tree branch or lamppost on that bright day

sky just greying at the edges now   edging
            building & bank into smoke   & blur & smudge—
                        no way to build sight but through sound   so listen:

                    the last light that stings the palm   palms that
        stretch   reach   ravel   rub
the day from the skin the brick   *hear it?*   from the lily the pulse the palm

                                                & now look up   look up:

aubade

to walk next to a river i. am listening. for the switch of.
starlings of. sunsets descending. on the mire on. the
spurs on a petrified. history. dark. the cypress dark. the
sight. of the tree. that bends to hold. the river i. am
walking next to

rivermists. they ache here how i. ache to swallow
bridges. with starlings. stranded in the bracing
embracing. the river

mists in fallacy. the wish for. a starling. a body is only.
a halved hymn. a startling. & doesn't it all. end here
with. a swelling a. sunrise a. weary aubade a. little
bloated with how i. want to remember the mists

that seep. over boots &. starlings i. can't swallow. the
river or. the mists or. the aspen as. it was dressed. in
leaves in. sleeping starlings

what is it you taste when you die in the night

the flecked spores of days pouring into crevices
                          between hill & fallen husk

                                                        between aspen & aspen

the tide
                          & the gulls' gulling   of sky
             with their calls to each   other with their catch
                                                    of plum pit

                                                              & prayer

             with their calls to wind

& lily & lighthouse & cliff &

                                                  there's never

                          quite the same feeling
             as moonlight on the back
of the thigh   slipping itself

                                                like tide over its pebbles
                                                like rat over greyashed leaves
                                                      fawn stirring, thrumming
             toward the clearing of grasses   & windbreath
it might all be

hearsay   it might

        all be the day & its minutes
its answers of pebbles   & wing

                                                      & etiquette trekked
over knotted hours & knotted barks   it might be the silver silt

in hardened lungs frosting breath   into glassy hoarfrost
        whisper   *vesper*

it might be all
              it is   all it is

                                                      is moonlight

homegrowths

a swift awakening of tongues, then quiet
                              a simmer underneath
of whittled folios, a perfect bind

                              to form a history
out of tridents, the quill must acquiesce
            against the rims of crystal glasses
                     we bequeathed the life of a lightning strike

i named the wind by the smokestack offerings:
                              a daily turbulence
from above, the bridge indicts the orient of the sun
            seeping estuary, unsought
                              our brackish mouths
                                        wide open & spitting

overgrown gums: a rotten cemetery,
            sleeping like the fading moon under the gullwing
amber light feathered   into tender marrow
            nutrientrings
                     swallowings

our pains are white & twiggy under the bright lights of these artifices
urban forestry, desexed   alone, i am a bayou porch
            rural birchbite
                     knees of aspen

when we replaced our fingers with topiaries,
the strength of mint stalks   became quantifiable
            spine devours extremities for their succulents
                     impeccable blastocysts

i forget, lately, how the body is   to carve wrists from petrified trunks
                 hair from ironlace
                     fifolets spark from marsh water, i watch
                                     as the baubles dance:

how the sun fidgets time into concentric circles & breathes back into itself

& today a hull to hold on to

let the body slip out of itself into
something tidy let the body silk
its way into hinge & delay
    hinge & hinge into some
thick threads of lilies

into the haunting lull of birches
& their expectancies the way air
bowhinged wrists around their
bodies the way their bodies
hinged bow to the shoulder &
the wrist

the way their skin splinters into
wingtip & bodies swarm with
fog: tender & firm
     & expectant

& when the air splinters with
sound with breath with the snap
of some ordinary tuesday what
then becomes of the body & its
lilies : what then becomes

of the birchbow the splinter &
the splintered lily : the artery &
the pact the wrist & its hinge the
tidings untidy the grip

gripping the lull lulling into
airtender breaths & eddies

the lessening into splitself &
song: here's after here's what's
after here's what it's like to be
after   to be

something lost & found its skin
again : to have something to
shiver in : to be the lily lifted at
the wrist : the birch

unhinging from breathsong : to
unthread &

stretched & expectant

to let the lilies linger

lilies & these eroded

& here there's something in the
lilies here & there & over that
way something

•

in the lilies the slick sienna
tongues of antlered stamen
anthers split to smudge the
white here right here & over

•

that way a lilied crush of shell
at the seaside crisp & tonguing

•

again & again here & over that
way

•

lilies at shoredge

•

weigh the phrase against its
foliage: so much vastness in
the gasping roots so much in
the gasping tides

•

here & over that way here &
over that way & here & here &
here &

•

tide a crush of lilies an unravel
a peel back lilies the tide
unfurling against its anthers
against it the tide it's here its
cold solid glass

•

its cold musics the way they're
made lilies & cylindrical shells
golden & ratioed synapse to
synapse lisped round the edges
licked eroded tongued out of
lilting seasong these lilies

•

here that it's this: phrase &
moment excerpt but not the
whole filaments plucked &

splayed a firmament of lily & lily
over that way it's all lilied
up hear it : phrase & root

•

here & over that way

•

here lilies here tide here the
lilies all tied in their glass
cages their tideswept stems
leaves all tidied up these lilies
these ones here & over &

•

here the tide's colicky terror:
lilies dripping every last rib
every spent petal that at some
point here & over that way it's

all lilies in the tide

•

that at some point the body
ends & stops beginning & stops
ending

•

that at some point it's all lilies
that at some point it's all here

•

& what does that make of any
preposterous, ecstatic love
before the body of water before
the body

•

of lilies

•

here lilies

here tide

•

& over that way

●

"the light flayed her she was a new woman she could inhabit a shape"
—Jorie Graham

from granite illusion, so the conjoined world follows

cento

the rims of wounds have wounds as well:
                              inside the name,   the trick
is to see things as they are: slick bark
tin can purged of all its minerals   a meadow of some suffering
                  some silk grief ago, before the cut
            of cinnamon or the linnet-colored
thinking which i try to seal off with a sentence, i invoke
                  her gathering figs

in the thieving,   working back & forth, a breach
            augments the meadow with its redness,   incessant scour of light
it is the gluttony of gravity, dazed
by its own mute replication   of wire & shadow & sound, obliterating
                  most of what's imagined growing there

the slim road dissolves   if we each dig
            back to our own tectonic shelf, entering   dark vowels, hollow—
symbol & source are what i mean
                              figs ripen from the inside out,
ocular weather is every kind, all times, all kinds   of strange beasts

to attend decay as it sets in:
                  a sky wrestling its dark
                        the mud out there hurrying to be ordinary
                                    after all night breathing ash

to heather is to stake a claim

while the sun thickens. its tools to. hunt the ground's nooks &. corners with. breath no. more than shadow. left hanging. at the cleft of throat &. hankering an. apex. of weather

at its winds its. withering its. rewinding fields of. heather into. *huff &. hurry huff. & hurry* to become. just a wreath of. patched hillside ripple of. impulse above thatching tilled. into cottage that. itches to break. free

a brave exit. aiming for what. it's always. been this lilting wind licking. seasons from. one eave to. roof to. glen iffy with. light & its. lastness to. tangent clasping. at springtime yes

it's springtime. the balance of. fresh heather belies the. treble. crevassing open. expanse of. something called *sky* called. *blue* called. *bright* & in. breachleaf. thereleaf there the feral. lip of. petal over stem of. nothing. to breathe

that's not. already been. seen that's not. already been
heaved knotted into. nervebent spine it. hurts every. time
this cursive winding. itself to tether to. heather. to claim
just. this sun &. somewhere close

some wear their bodies. like music. their oncethudded
atoms slick with. others' bluffs a. compass for. every
spinecracked song a. bare bird with. bones that. twitch
at. the briskness of

something. to remember. a map of. springtime a. day
with. something to. want. to be. let free to. be let free &.
dying to have. stopped questioning the. churn of things
already. abandoned

:

cross your legs uncross your legs cross your legs uncross your legs cross your legs uncross your legs

amnesty

the lady was not offering & so
      they dissembled: sapphire-tongued growths stretching
        for aftermath   & the lady steeps tea

                          from lavender skeins
     to remember how to weep the skin
        raw deaths of the dried stalks   & pleasured barrows

a falter
        a falter

after the breaths cool
     the afternets   exclaiming in their bounty
       how personal the sky

once you've slept under it
       ask the lady   ask her
                    ask her how she takes her tea

:

along these synaptic passages a little light
      a little light never did anyone anything good
      perhaps

a little light never did
      except
the plum tree

․

with or without these luminosities no orchard's complete
　　　without a body to plum　　　　　　*legs to kick*　　　　　*crossuncross*
　　　　　hands　　　*or branches*

standard practice

the meshed emblem i place. into its own weaknesses
my. weakness my. mug my. tea my plums husky above.
the lavender. skeins dissembling into. scented mesh.

scenting every. chainlink fence with. dusk &. weeping
skin wrung. beside gulls & velvet ritual of. swarm &
stretch of. dismay of. every. teastained missive sent every

where slendering the knee its. apostrophes its. steamed
glass seeping. out of courtesy & a case made. for desire
for. the space between wrists for. lilies mottled. at the
throat & wearing. themselves slender where

birchskins accumulate into. music into. apostrophes
filling. the husks of. abandoned pianos. their repetitions
dusty & littered. with lilies with. little rituals with.
lavender juices. plumlight & faltering over. skins &
birches buried

up to the throat the. emblem meshing & breathcaught
breaching &. beseech it. beseech it falling. across glassy
light. beseech it falling across. the knee & all its soft
things. beseech the mesh &. the throat

&. its practical breezes its. ravenous rituals beseech it &
its every weaknesses

urban planning when prayers for the body aren't enough

i am walking out   of footprints
body left behind in crystals, i am
walking here next to rusted wires, a fester left behind

where you once built a city
of bodies on Sundays, structures: lilies
            lawns: palmpressed & praying

there, we spun whistles into anthems
      peeled off scabs   to watch the clots pearl

& what's the point of bridges anyway,
      hovering over nothing
            more than their marrow

            over this rucksack of riches,
    pearls unspooled   & pooling
& this city crystal underfoot

      on days like this,
it's nice to remember how it feels
            away from the sentence filled like a city

:

along these synaptic passages a weak signal hello   cross your legs
uncross your legs   a quick electrical fix   cross your
          uncross your   the dripping drive to move something   legs
          silky tendons   or think

billow & pulse

what vertebra's the one that makes the tide tremble. saltspined & ringed in gold threads. tipsy with light & iron at the throat.

here in the in betweens this body all styled with wildflowers. with lilies. phosphorescent under sunmurk. the body the bridge with its tendons. all aglint. all a simmering dimglow.

hard things & soft things. hard things & soft things. hard things & soft things & spongesilt in the riverbed. how to tend to the body when all that's left is what's made to bristle. to settle in.

•

along the crestline, crushed
oystershells. & within the lungs
a pearl. when the air is an
allergy what's left but to stretch
it into unexistence. the
unraveling into its grey matter &
softening—

here the body made of all these
gold threads grey now
dimmering & dimmer. beds of
something nettled across
floodmarked calves & pockets
of electric blessings. here,
bless. here, bless. here, river
that knows to contain itself in
neon.

& to contain. to unwrap itself
around its boundaries & warp
itself over. spine split down the
middle & peeled open. what's
left of the self when the self is
what's left & there's no light to
see by. & always leaning.

•

glisten & glimmerslipped. into
curve & clayshape. where is the
tide not seeping. crawling itself
over pebble & silt. hard things
& soft things. hard things & soft
things. hard things & soft things
all underskinned.

what's the curve of the knee
without the wrist to mirror it.
what's left to summon. the
ceiling of the river. the sealing
of the tide. in the dark the
hunger for the boundary. for the
rule to abide by. what
weightlessness in the throat
when there's nothing to
swallow. to choke on.

even in the measuring in the
measured breath the vertebra
ties itself with the tidings of
what's been & been again. the
path now open. the gate now
breached. bankless under itself
& overing. time is what's
spoken & what's missed.

•

lidded or lifted, can't see the
salt or the blooming. not a
vertebral   difference.
tendonbridged & what's left to
question of it. the body & all its
soft things. skinhungering for
what's willed at the wrist. what
will it. what it will.

threads & tipsed & flowerfaced
around its irons.

—no. with nothing to see by but
fingerprint & hairlilt the body is
made of eyes all over. beacon
& brimming. selfsustaining into
will & what's next. the rivering?
blanketworld wrapped its arms
around? hard things & soft
things. hard things & soft things
this body's becomed. . .

saltstarched & sunken & in
every water rerounded. & in
every tongue—

the sea thinks beyond itself

slowskulled   & drowsy,
this epitaph's   the one that's carved
over   & over again :
here a blowsy   mallet & chisel
to chisel

             on the rock   this tide's
overswept   in looking
too close   for tidings for   how to remain
unwaving   unwavering
the shore   it's always
                      the depths
itself   tense & feathering &
not about itself   & counting
the time   it takes to linger
where it's not
wanted   here waking it's
the same   rock
that's waiting   to be
             to have   one more
drink to quench
             this ebony   shore -
fight :
             tide   throat
       tide
           tide
                throat

on speech

the pebbles at the beach's bottom drown & are rebreathed
each tide   like the human body's slipping sleepward & jolting back
                 & back: a rest that's never true & a wake that's all gasp

& release. we don't remember
how to catch breath & shape it   bubble-soft & trailing
                          into something to care for, to ear after
instead, airbound, we gulp quickly   giddy at the glottal
                          teeth tense   stifling in breath

as lungs inflate   exhale
                          a flight like a gull on the updraft   *is this exhilaration?*
          suck & gasp   lips pressed to windburst
                          the gall of it

                 trapping what's invisible   into mouthshape   tongue swaddled tight
against billow & blessing   & we don't remember
                                                             we don't remember
our primary tasks as the pebbles sink into sand & seaswoon

we hang our jaws open by the molar in wait

                                                  the air here hangs

just as lightless in our caves & cavities   tiding itself

into cheeks & out   it doesn't want to be swallowed
                & it doesn't want to be let go
                & it fills our mouths with its cacophonies
                                      echo & original sound
sometimes

we kick the pebbles at the beach's bottom but only
when sun's alchemy
                turns them silvered & slivering   we're afraid

of letting them slip   into nightness & we're afraid of them
bleakdamp   sifting speech across our surfaces

        they too closely resemble
                        our own clammy souls   slowly
overcome
                with tide

                                        it's brittle in our mouths

this dusty light

                              our cheeks

         full of pebbles

                              & aglow

:

cross your legs uncross your legs cross your legs uncross your legs saltgulled into
     quick electrical synapse   *drylight &*   *crystalled*
       cross your   *legs*   *uncross your*   *legs*

what else to do but this

& when the fog itself
                        was full of wildflowers

a cheshire evening   the lady wrapped herself into

•

no breezes   just
                         wildflowers

                                             at the throat
                                             at the tide

•

the lady's throat
                         a catching net
               foggy

surging with
                wildflowers   their names

•

the wildflowers   the sea

emptying themselves against its knees

casual gifts   for the lady

•

the lady   her gifts

                      a decade of onyx
luminesced at the wrist

•

at the wrist   tidelight, annexed
                                   wildflowers, annexed

      the pulpy frothing
                     of justplucked salts sifted
                                 from shore & stem

•

the lady enstems her wildflowers

         —why wait for something gold & growing—

•

enropes her wildflowers

—*opens their mouths*—

enraptures

•

& pushes in its anthers

—*the lady*—
—*& pushes in*—

their pulsing decadences

their anthems

:

dried out or prickling along these synaptic passages   *salt's not a*
touchstone   *for a long season*

preservation tactics

orange, how it festers:
a stomach, digesting itself   into platoons
of orange trees, orange leaves

you count crevices of your palms
secret ferns, nothing   but a pithy city

                                              i'm dreaming

about landscapes i've never seen, a node
                of wildflowers, blooming into fever,
                a city built of bodies, bodies of ferns

the ferns are whispering orange,   shifting
for the humidity   of the shelled soil like
                palms, hundreds of   palms
building cities like handprints

an orange, plucked, a fester, a fist—
we eat dead things to stay alive

from the birches

democracy of. swollen. things receiving in. doubt the roots
below. mistake the branch before. the flower. turns

•

we have been elected. electric we have. been dealt a
lectern of. lilies. something.

•

to tell you we. have been. magnetized out of. rushes. the
river a. hectic. husband.

•

we crystalled into. two lilies. today blushing. a
fluorescent wild. flower a. humbling tumble. ahem.
ahem. we do not.

•

mean to hide. our laughter here. a mile. after the sinew
pulled. a perfect dusk. we do not love. you but we.

must. ask for your wrists.

:

we give things our names   along these synaptic passages   to understand
        them better   cross   along these synaptic   passages
how many spines   uncross   are not our spines   cross
                skins   uncross   eyes

sanctuary

there are beads on the iron bars
                          framing these streets we walk
these streets lead us to the cemetery
              where we are prohibited

from walking   & there are beads   on these headstones
          so we look closer   these names
tell stories of the voodoo gangs
                                        & behind,
              their misspelled families   who toss baubles

                                        & don't look
to see where they land   it's this history   this
          omen   starling
is what keeps us roaming the rows
                                  under the swollen throat
of the warbling bird on the treebranch

                                        one flit away from the rotten hive
              left hanging
          i'm told to prefer the earthly thing: lilies
rising   from clots of freshly turned earth   but they're just
              blooming
the bodies beneath them

                              petals of marrow
                              stems that stretch from hair follicles
              & sway a little   in the breeze
that's no breath of any living thing   the tree on the left
              has shriveled into bark & a cavity,

                                                  a place to hide,

but on these streets everything's invisible   but the body
      you ask me about a thought   & i tell you that

        to starling

             is to burst open & envelop

on these streets   is the offer of a buoy:
        we are walking through
        this after-hours death

& the sunset is heading   in the right direction
      i tell you about   a plot
        somewhere,   in an aging mausoleum,
        & i really mean not one

but many: different bodies,   different mysteries
      you set the pace   & pretend to mean it
a spectral worry empties the dusk,

      & there is satisfaction in finding   a loose stone

            & slipping a little

:

how many necks not ours   the bottle   the body of water

out of pebbles

tesseract the tendrils of heather. hedgerow links lanes into an unruly alphabet. its letters, the cleft of the bayou. the cleft of the bayou acts

its letters. it's lettering in "pretty." & meaning it. without condensing. the body into something to ask for: its hard things & soft things. all. of its polished vertebrae. the bayou lets

the body unearth. the dripped skins. of birch trees if. it is too. daring then. what are we even doing here. what's left. of the gritty. heather mud silking down. the knee. of the field. what we've been. seeking. the breezes & the pebbles & the plum tree. the borders of a body. that pleases. throat. strummed into lily—

& tonight this is what it's like

for the heart to be so hardy so
full the body brims over itself &
slips   foolhardy   out   the
skinsheen : ghosts billow out
the husks of stomachs into a
duel with the air their own
individual weathers

& in the day that's smaller than
the things we're carrying this is
what it's like to be full of lilies
full of these living tongues that
bring forth ghost after ghost : a
spectrum of slipshod thistles &
drums a little different under the
surface

so : to unearth the rendering of
these verbal spaces the fusses

at hand a little need to think
about what the wristwrapped
questions lend themselves to : a
discussion at the lectern at the
knee a question at most a little
tender a little lost in its
unraveling

& this is what it's like to be alive
when everyone's talking about
the night & its heights & you
know what it's like to stalk
starlings & bully hunger into its
hurting & to wake up with the
tide & its aches

this is also what it's like to be the
visible   space   of   what's
hiding   of   what   you've
destroyed & now lilied you
carry each day even on the day
when you're busy counting
hues careening off the cheek &
heeding its flushings to know

this is not this day
anymore

& this is what it's like to have a
pull heckling the left knee & on
nights when the heart gets full
like this is this what it's like

to be ribboned into honest
flickerings to be full of these
lilies full of these small things
years & dates & you & tonight
i'm so happy : wrists tumbled
all together knees ripping the
cage of them the falter the
release & what's left but a small
step outside

the skin all breezehumbled
with ghosts & kin & this is what
night feels when the stars
haven't come out yet but

what's left of the thinning
daysun still warm on the
forearm & this is what it's like to
know the stars are just up there
waiting to yawn with tide &
aching to wake up

notes

Before sharing some informational notes on certain poems, I'd like to explore some structural thoughts. When I say "I," here, I'm no longer the "i" of the poems, the speaker-i, the poetic "i." Instead, here I am: author-I. I want to break down the poetic fourth wall and offer some thoughts on the world of *night myths*, the world I've had inside me for so many years. This, perhaps, is one of the most intimate moments—one of the most conspiratorial. Come on in—to our world. Let's break down its structural integrity.

night myths is divided at a central hinge, "lilies & these eroded." This meditation functions both as the vertex of the book's "v" and as the nadir of the speaker's emotional self-consideration. The aphelion of the speaker's mental orbit. How many metaphors can I apply in one paragraph? Hah. Let's add one more: the Petrarchan volta, the turn to the sestet's fresh perspective. But instead of a true turn, I think of this moment as a refraction, the point at which the speaker begins to operate at a slightly different frequency. All the various selves of the poems are the same selves, but redirected, reconsidered. Isn't that what growth is, anyway? It's this moment where the same speakers pivot to see themselves in new light—pun intended—and so can *become* new as a result.

Both body sections open with poems that lift up found language (see those specific poem notes below). This is a first book, my first book, and as a result contains perhaps the purest accumulation and consideration of poetic influence. I don't mean "influence" as a bad thing. We all come from somewhere. We're all informed by the work we read, the conversations we have, the people we meet. The found language at the top of each section attempts to honor that history. I couldn't have written this book, my first book, without everything I've been exposed to along the way.

Each body section concludes with a poem set apart from the rest. These cousin-poems, this not-quite-a-matching-set, have two functions. Materially, they serve as an anti-poem, a dénouement, an epilogue to the series of experiences that came before. They are the synthesis of the bodies that precede them. Structurally, they function as a parallel to the found poems at their sections' openings. They attempt to merge their poetic history with their own selfhood. I use "attempt" here intentionally, as this work is work I will be considering and revisiting over and over again. So, I suppose what I'm saying is that at its heart, *night myths* is an origin story. My origin story. My becoming. Thank you for becoming with me.

•

"a long vulnerability of paper & consciousness": This is a found poem whose language comes from the show "/what are we but lying single surface/," which ran at The Alice gallery in Seattle, Washington, from October 14 through November 18, 2017. I was the gallery's writer-in-residence for the duration of the show, which explored "themes of identity, place, family, language, collaboration, and self-making"—themes that became intrinsic to the considerations and structures of *night myths*. The visual and literary artists featured in this exhibition include Vickie Vértiz, Kenji C. Liu, Gutta' Collective members Joel Salcido and Rashaad Thomas, Kerry Downey, and Katherine Simóne Reynolds. The Alice, which closed in 2019, was run by incredibly talented folks, including Natalie Martínez and Molly Mac. The language of this poem includes fragments from the works themselves as well as the formal exhibition notes.

"particular reminders when prayers for the body aren't enough": This poem originated during a free-write I conducted during my visits to The Alice (see additional detail on that above). I sat on the wood floor and spent a series of five to ten minutes facing each wall, so I could observe and be in as much of the art as possible.

"aubade": I created "aubade" to honor the memory of Hunter Deely, who's literary life goal was to become "one of the all-time greats." Hunter passed in 2012, and his work is memorialized in issue ten of *THERMOS*. This poem owes many of its images to Hunter's work and hopes to celebrate them anew.

"& today a hull to hold on to": This poem is for Ian Gallagher Zelazny. Ian was a writer, thinker, philosopher, friend. He was always amazed by others' poems and liked exploring abandoned places. Ian died in 2012.

"from granite illusion, so the conjoined world follows": As noted in the epigraph of the poem, this is a cento, built with lines from (in order of appearance, but not noting repetitions): Lucie Brock-Broido, Anna Rabinowitz, Amaranth Borsuk, Karla Kelsey, Jorie Graham, Laura Walker, and Karen Volkman. The title of this poem is itself its own cento, comprised of words from the book titles where these lines were borrowed.

"the sea thinks beyond itself": I wrote the early version of this poem via a free-write I made immediately following reading Brian Teare's *Companion Grasses*, which considers place, humanity, and the musics that connect the two.

"on speech": This poem first found its legs after creating and testing a poem map of Traci Brimhall's "The Summer after They Crashed and Drowned," from her book *Rookery*. I made this poem map and initial poem draft while standing at the counter in Open Books: A Poem Emporium, Seattle's poetry-only bookstore.

"sanctuary": This poem is the result of following a prompt from Andy Stallings and the expansive logic of Blaise Cendrars. The prompt involved connecting poems with movement, in this case, a walk. At the time, I was living in New Orleans, and my walk took place in the Garden District. I then returned to my notebook and conducted a free-write, which became the early language of this poem.

"& tonight this is what it's like": This poem is for neither speaker-i nor author-I. It's for the self-I. The self I was, the self I have been, the self I am. It's a meditation and an exaltation. It's a memory. A reminder. It's a promise.

ACKNOWLEDGMENTS

I can't begin to describe the immense honor I feel at being able to write these acknowledgments. It means that *night myths* exists, is on its way to existing in a form outside of the Word doc on my computer. I also know that it takes—has taken—will continue to take—a village.

Names hold meaning, hold power. I'd like to share some names here.

I am immeasurably grateful to Red Hen Press for their belief in me and my work. Kate, Mark, Tobi, Monica, Rebeccah, Shelby, Chloë, Amanda, Marc, Megan, Yoshi, Piper: thank you for seeing my work and backing me, for opening your literary home to me. You have changed my life.

I'd also like to acknowledge the homes of pieces that came before the whole, the places that welcomed bits of what would become *night myths*. Thank you to the following journals, whose editors said yes to these works, sometimes in earlier shapes or forms:

    antiphony: "to heather is to stake a claim"
    Bayou Magazine: "the hearth no longer a hallowed frame   i found"
    Broadsided Press: "island sided"
    Crab Creek Review: "what is it you taste when you die in the night"
    Cream City Review: "to forest is to hide a woman"
    CutBank: "from granite illusion, so the conjoined world follows"
    Denver Quarterly: "a walk in the woods"
    EcoTheo Review: "aubade"
    EX/POST: "standard practice"
    Foundry: "lilies & these eroded"
    Guernica: "preservation tactics"
    H_NGM_N: "& today a hull to hold on to" (as "a lesson in decomposing"), "homegrowths," "wildflower mythology"
    Inch: "out of pebbles"
    Jack Straw Writers' Anthology: all interspersed stanzas (as "body mythlets")
    Janus Head: "billow & pulse" (meadow)
    Poetry Northwest: "7:28PM: above the river the bridge   the bridge"
    The Birds We Piled Loosely: "amnesty," "from the birches" (as "democracy of swollen things")
    The Seattle Review of Books: "if the mirror," "urban planning when prayers for the body aren't enough," "the sea thinks beyond itself," "to live in ignorance is exactly what"
    The Shore: "billow & pulse" (tide), "& today a hull to hold on to," "& tonight this is what it's like"
    The Spectacle: "the auction," "what else to do but this" (as "stains of an enemy's century")

Thank you to the organizations that supported me at key moments in the creation of *night myths*: AWP, Jack Straw Cultural Center, Hugo House, Poetry Northwest Editions, *The Seattle Review of Books*, The Alice, Open

Books: A Poem Emporium. Your rooms (both tangible and virtual) offered me space, breath, and care, all of which I tenderly needed.

To the academic institutions and the people therein who nourished and guided me, thank you. At the University of Washington, Richard Kenney, Pimone Triplett, Andrew Feld, and Linda Bierds. You taught me to think, to push the line between mystery and clarity. And my fellow writers near-and-during that time: Patrick Milian, Catherine Bresner, Adriana Campoy, Alison Stagner, Justine Chan, Alex Streim, Kristin Gulotta, Erin L. McCoy, Rachel Edelman, Gabrielle Bates, Michelle Hope Anderson, Lauren Schleshinger, Jane Youngberg. Here's to you, to your words, to the footsteps we took together to find our own ways into writing, and to the ways in which each of you helped shape my own. At Tulane University, to Peter Cooley, who offered the wisdom that transformed what I thought writing poetry was. To Andy Stallings, who cracked open what language could do. And to your poetry workshops, my first poetry workshops, especially the one of spring 2012: the purest synergy, the most earnest and necessary belief.

The act of putting pen on paper is individual, but writing exists in community. To my community, thank you: C. R. Grimmer, you're kind of replaceable (too soon?). Laura Da', Joyce Chen, Shelby Handler, Piper Lane, Sasha taqʷšəblu LaPointe, Jen Soriano, Kristen Millares Young—you are the definition of self-advocacy, of empowerment. #gushguts4eva. Kristen, it's an honor to be your pressmate and your friend, to see how you forge your way. I would not be here without your asking "why not?" and "what if?". Sarah Suhr, our Tuesday ritual. Woogee Bae, all the earl grey cupcakes. Katelyn Oppegard, paper folds and your Virgo soul. CAWK lyfe. Cody Stetzel—count the almonds. Keetje Kuipers and my poetry gals (Rachel Edelman, Gabrielle Bates), you hold me to time, to task, and to trueness (to myself, to the work). E. J. Koh, the attention and intention you devote to every moment. Katie Lee Ellison, for asking the right questions. Jay Aquinas Thompson, one more Café Presse chocolat chaud for the road. Melissa Dickey, my New Orleans poetry gurl, and to all of our gurls near and far. Kevin Craft, for all the collaboration, all the books. Susan Rich, for unending generosity and encouragement. Emily Stoddard, you create a positive ripple effect that touches so many lives, mine included. Rosebud Ben-Oni, key thoughts at a key moment—I am forever grateful. Wendy Barnes, you push me to unlock what's possible and turn all of my lists (and spreadsheets, and bullet points) into action.

R, my heart, my home: you teach me the meaning of bravery. Of kindness. Of strength through gentleness. Thank you for seeing all of my selves, for believing in me, from the beginning.

To my dad, Arky. We never got to dream this together. The Sketchers don't exist, the Dodges don't exist, but this book—this moment—does.

Finally, thank you to my mom, Lori, a woman who has shown me time and time again that becoming yourself is a journey, is not a straight line. It's the most powerful thing you can do. Thank you for showing me the way.

Biographical Note

Abi Pollokoff is a poet, editor, and book artist. Her work has appeared in publications such as *TriQuarterly*, *Denver Quarterly*, and *Guernica*, and in such installations as the Summit Sound, the Seattle Convention Center sound installation. Abi was named a 2021 Jack Straw Writer and a 2019 Hugo Fellow. She has held residencies from the *Seventh Wave*, the *Seattle Review of Books*, and the Alice Gallery. In 2012, Abi won the Anselle M. Larson/Academy of American Poets Prize for Tulane University, judged by Caryl Pagel. She was a finalist for the 2022 Coniston Prize, judged by Dorianne Laux, and the 2022 Gatewood Prize, judged by Julie Carr, and a semifinalist for the 2021 Lexi Rudnitsky First Book Prize. Her poem "aubade" was a finalist for the 2019 Omnidawn Broadside Contest, judged by Dan Beachy-Quick. In addition to her own writing, Abi is the managing editor of Poetry Northwest Editions and works in publishing. Abi received her MFA in poetry from the University of Washington. She lives in Brooklyn, New York, by way of Seattle, New Orleans, and the Chicagoland area. Find her at abipollokoff.com.